Committee Clearance of

Administrative Decisions

Committee Clearance

of

Administrative Decisions

William E. Rhode

BUREAU OF SOCIAL AND POLITICAL RESEARCH
Michigan State University: College of Business and Public Service

Library of Congress Catalog Card Number: 59-62974

ACKNOWLEDGMENTS

I would like to take this opportunity to express my appreciation to several persons who played an important role in the completion of this study. First, I would like to express my thanks to Professor Glendon A. Schubert, Michigan State University. As a teacher, Professor Schubert stimulated my interest in the topic of committee clearance; as a colleague and friend, he offered suggestions and encouragement. Secondly, I would like to thank Professor Norton E. Long, who, as Acting Director of the Governmental Research Bureau, Michigan State University, made it possible for me to spend two weeks in Washington, D. C., gathering invaluable data and material. Professor Frank A. Pinner, present Director of the Bureau of Social and Political Research, also deserves a special vote of thanks. This work owes a great deal to his constructive criticisms and personal suggestions. To a very large extent, this study rests upon the gracious cooperation and assistance of many staff members of congressional committees and officers in executive agencies at the nation's capital. Data which otherwise would have been unobtainable were gathered in interviews with these persons. Each of them interrupted a busy schedule to give freely and willingly of his time and attention. Last, but certainly not least, I would like to express my gratitude to Miss Carol Cotton and Miss Astrid Eriksson, students at San Diego State College, who spent a great deal of time typing several manuscript drafts. Needless to say, none of these persons is responsible for any errors of fact or interpretation.

TABLE OF CONTENTS

I
INTRODUCTION

The past century has been a period of great changes in
American society and government. One of the most
significant and far-reaching of such changes has been
the explosive expansion of the national bureaucracy.
The President and Congress of pre-Civil War America
could easily keep watch over an administrative organization small in size and simple in structure. In today's
industrial society the national administration is a far
cry from this historical model. Bureaucracy has come
to be a major institution of a complex society which
requires the services of over two million people and
costs the taxpayers many millions of dollars.[1] A huge,
sprawling network of departments, agencies, and bureaus
has spread out over the United States and has reached
into foreign countries.

---

1.   See Tax Foundation, Inc., **Facts and Figures on Govern-
      ment Finance**, 10th edition, 1958-1959, p. 33.

Accompanying this tremendous growth there have been ever increasing needs and pressures to place broad discretionary authority in the hands of the national bureaucracy. Administrative discretion has become one of the prominent features of our modern-day American national government. Indeed, administrative discretion has become so fundamental in the governmental process that, in its absence, it would be very difficult to transform policy decisions and pronouncements into successful and operative governmental programs. Whether it be the implementation of major policies in the field of national security or the execution of a governmental program of postoffice construction, administrative discretion has become a key feature of the process. Without it our twentieth-century government would become a paralyzed giant unable to perform its many tasks.

This growth of administrative discretion has not resulted from any sinister designs of power-hungry administrators. Industrialization, two foreign wars, a major economic depression, the emergence of strong pressure groups demanding protection and promoting their interests, and many other factors have led to a vast extension of the responsibilities placed on the shoulders of the national government. Governmental programs and activities have grown accordingly. The new and enlarged role of the national government has, in turn, heightened the importance and expanded the functions of administrative discretion.

This movement toward the extensive reliance on delegated discretionary powers has, in recent decades, posed an especially serious problem for the United States Congress. In order to set up programs that would meet the demands and responsibilities thrust upon a government of a modern industrial society, the legislative body has been forced to turn over large chunks of its powers to the administrative branch. At the same time, however, it has been growing increasingly apparent in

the halls of Congress that effective legislative control over the uses of such powers cannot be insured
through traditional devices in the hands of the legislative
body.

A brief look at the traditionally accepted methods of
congressional control over administration will show
this. For example, it has been generally believed that
the legislature can closely channel and guide the use of
discretionary authority by encasing its grants of powers
in a rigid framework of principles and standards. Increasingly, this view has come to be regarded as un-
realistic. Administrative agencies in all fields of
governmental activity have had to deal with evermore
complex and rapidly changing situations; they have
demanded--and obtained--standards less rigid and more
general in scope. Such loosely circumscribed grants
of authority, necessarily allowing a great deal of room
for alternative decisions and actions by an agency, have
greatly reduced the possibilities of satisfactory prenatal congressional control over administrative action.

There are other tools of surveillance in the legislative
repertory, such as the annual budget review, deriving
from the appropriation power vested in Congress, and
periodic hearings by regular standing committees and
special investigating committees. The limited effective-
ness of these tools is quite obvious. At most, they can
serve as periodic checks upon past uses of delegated
authority and as attempts to reorient future exercises of
discretionary powers. They cannot insure Congress of
a voice in the specific, day-to-day uses of the powers
Congress has turned over to the administrative branch.
But as the need to make broad and general grants of
authority to the administrative agencies becomes more
pressing, the only meaningful method of congressional
control is supervision over just such particular exercises
of administrative discretion.

This development has been a bitter pill for Congress to swallow. The legislative body has been traditionally sensitive about the growth of administrative power, which it has often viewed as bureaucratic aggrandizement, and throughout history it has demanded a strong voice in the way such power was exercised. It is easy to see why the modern-day necessity to delegate broad, sweeping discretionary authority to the executive branch, coupled with the increasing ineffectiveness of the normal control devices, has produced a feeling of frustration and concern on Capitol Hill.

This situation has prompted Congress in recent years to search for new and more effective supplementary tools of supervision and oversight. One of the products of this search has been the development of a unique method to superintend the uses of the administrative discretion turned over to the administrative hierarchy. This new tool is committee clearance of administrative decisions, or, more simply, committee clearance.

Committee clearance is based on the requirement that decisions of executive departments and subordinate agencies which constitute proposed uses of discretionary authority delegated by Congress be reviewed by a congressional committee prior to their execution. The departments and agencies are directed to submit the decisions to specified committees for review and study. Committee approval validates the decisions and allows the proposed use of delegated authority to become effective. Disapproval by the committee, on the other hand, nullifies the administrative decision. Committee clearance thus serves as an instrument for a prenatal type of legislative supervision and control over the specific, day-to-day uses of delegated discretionary powers by the executive branch.

This device was first used in the late 1920's when it was introduced as a means of legislative control over tax

4

refunds of the Internal Revenue Bureau. It was not until the Second World War, however, that it began to be a fairly regular tool of government. Since that time it has been employed on several occasions. Quite often it has been used to supervise the vast and far-flung real estate activities of the national military establishment. Similarly, administrative decisions carrying out government policies ranging from the acquisition of public buildings to the protection of wildlife sanctuaries have been subject to prior committee approval.

The pattern of use during the last decade and a half indicates that committee clearance is well on its way to becoming a permanent addition to the system of congressional control over administration. In spite of this development, however, the device has apparently attracted little attention among students of American government and has yet to be subjected to a detailed and comprehensive examination.[2] This is regrettable because the new development raises basic issues that deserve discussion and analysis by the academic community.

---

2. The only published works dealing with this device are: Robert W. Ginnane, "The Control of Federal Administration by Congressional Resolutions and Committees," Harvard Law Review, LXVI (February, 1953), 569-611, and Cotter, Cornelius P., and Smith, J. Malcolm. "Administrative Accountability: Reporting to Congress," Western Political Quarterly, X (June, 1957), 405-415. Part of one chapter of an unpublished Ph.D. dissertation also discusses committee clearance. See Kenneth Theodore Kofmehl, "Congressional Staffing, with Emphasis on the Professional Staff," (Ph.D. dissertation, Columbia University [microfilm date, 1956], University Microfilms, Ann Arbor, Michigan, Publication No. 17.063), pp. 206-223. A more complete coverage of this topic can be found in another unpublished dissertation: William E. Rhode, "Congressional Review of Administrative Decision-Making by Committee Clearance and Resolutions," (Michigan State University Library, 1958).

For instance, there is a serious question as to whether committee clearance satisfies the constitutional prescriptions concerning the relationships between the administrative branch, the Presidency, and Congress. Equally basic is the question whether committee clearance promotes responsible administration, a principle at the core of American administrative theory and of the philosophy of American democracy. The impact of committee clearance upon the relationship between the President and his administrative subordinates is still another problem that should be explored.

Each of these issues merits attention and concentrated study. But such analyses can be undertaken only after a thorough understanding of American experience with committee clearance. At the present time no detailed and comprehensive picture of such experience is available. Designed to fill this gap, this study provides the first full discussion of the history and operation of committee clearance. Opening with a survey and analysis of the establishment and use of committee clearance from its inception in the late 1920's through 1957, it moves on to what is the first published account of the actual operation of this device. In the final chapter, devoted to an evaluation of the device, we discuss the question whether committee clearance has a legitimate place in our system of government.

A final word must be said about the data upon which this study is based. The greater share of the published source material was gathered from various official government documents. The annual volumes of the United States Statutes at Large from 1930 through 1956 were searched in order to obtain a listing of the instances in which committee clearance was established by statute. The legislative history of each piece of legislation containing the requirement of prior committee approval and the congressional debates preceding such legislative enactments were obtained from the United States Congressional Record. Finally, the Federal Register and many House and Senate committee reports furnished important sources of additional relevant data.[3]

---

3. The data concerning committee clearance in 1957 were obtained from recent research carried out by Professor Joseph Harris, University of California, Berkeley. Professor Harris gathered this information for a section in his forthcoming publication on legislative-executive relations, and he was kind enough to make his research findings available for use in this study.

II
FORMAL COMMITTEE CLEARANCE

There are two technically distinguishable types of committee oversight of administrative decision-making. We
shall call them "formal" and "informal" committee
clearance. The distinction refers to the manner in
which the requirement of prior committee approval is
established. In many instances the requirement of committee clearance has been imposed by a statute passed
by the Congress and signed by the President; such statutory requirements underlie what is here labeled "formal"
committee clearance. In other cases, however, the
requirement has been established by an informal agreement between an executive agency and a congressional
committee, or else it has developed out of a statutory
requirement that merely directs "prior reporting" of
proposed administrative decisions to particular committees before final action is taken; "informal" committee
clearance is the descriptive term for those situations in
which a prior approval arrangement is set up in one or
the other of these two latter ways.

8

As a practical matter, of course, this is a formal distinction. In the final analysis both types of clearance have a similar effect. In either case the administrative decisions are submitted to the reviewing committees in the form of proposals for the use of discretionary authority vested in the executive agency, and the committees retain the power of approval or disapproval. In either case, the result is always to place the ultimate control of administrative discretion in the hands of committees of the legislative body.

While the two types of committee clearance are indistinguishable in their effects, it is nevertheless interesting to observe the historical factors which make for their emergence. For this reason, this study considers them separately. The present chapter will focus on "formal" committee clearance. The next chapter will deal with the instances of "informal" committee clearance.

Formal Committee Clearance
-

The earliest example of formal clearance can be found in a naval public works statute passed in 1944.[4] This statute authorized the Secretary of the Navy to establish and develop naval shore facilities by acquiring and disposing of land and constructing necessary public works. The proposed acquisition and disposal of land for such facilities, however, could become effective only after review and approval by the naval affairs committees of Congress. A general proviso included in this statute declared, in reference to real estate activities of the Navy Department:

That prior to the acquisition or disposal, by

---

4.   U.S., Statutes at Large, LVIII, Part 1, 189

lease or otherwise, of any land acquired for naval use under the authority of this, or any other Act, the Secretary of the Navy shall come into agreement with the Naval Affairs Committees of the Senate and of the House of Representatives with respect to the terms of such prospective acquisitions or disposals.[5]

According to Representative Vinson, this requirement was written into the statute at that time in order to provide a system of authorization that would meet the strategical requirements of the Navy Department during the war emergency while at the same time maintaining congressional control over the real estate activities of that department. The needs for acquiring, and disposing of, land tended to arise suddenly as requirements for naval shore facilities shifted and changed rapidly to meet military necessities. Flexibility was crucially important, and control of land transactions by the usual method of itemized and detailed authorizations and appropriations covering a fairly long future period would have prevented such necessary flexibility. The device of committee clearance was thus intended to yield both the needed flexibility and the desired congressional control. Broad discretion[6] was delegated to the Navy Department with

---

5.   U.S., Statutes at Large, LVIII, Part 1, 190. This represents the first of several such requirements, both formal and informal, concerning the real estate and construction activities of the military establishment. The majority of instances of congressional committee review have related to the armed services departments and the Department of Defense, and, in most such cases, involved the activities mentioned above.

6.   The Secretary of the Navy was authorized to acquire the necessary land for various classes of projects of naval shore facilities. There was no specification in terms of location or particular facility. See U.S., Statutes at Large, LVIII, Part 1, 189.

the stipulation that the particular uses of this discretion have to be approved in each instance by the naval affairs committees of Congress. As Vinson explained, "we have done two things in this bill: We have given flexibility and we have tried to retain control over the acquisition and disposition of property."[7]

This statutory requirement, as it related to land acquisition, actually only wrote into law an informal arrangement that had existed for over a year regarding the acquisition of property by the Department of the Navy.[8] Secretary of the Navy Frank Knox and the House Committee on Naval Affairs, by an agreement in 1942, established a clearance procedure whereby all acquisitions of land by the Navy Department would become effective only upon approval by the naval affairs committees of Congress.[9] This agreement was kept for two years and

---

7. U.S., Congressional Record, 78th Cong., 2d Sess., 1944, XC, Part 3, 3218.

8. Kofmehl states: "This merely wrote into the law a clearance procedure which the Navy Department had been observing voluntarily for over a year--according to John J. Courtney, original draftsman of Public Law 289, 78th Congress, who at the time was on loan from the Justice Department to the Navy Department for the express purpose of handling the latter's real estate transactions (interview with Mr. Courtney on July 1, 1952)." Kofmehl, op. cit., supra, Chapter One, n. 2, p. 218, n. 28.

9. Representative Vinson, during debate on a bill in 1951, said: "Back in 1942 and 1943 an agreement was entered into by the old Committee on Naval Affairs with the Administration and with the then Secretary of the Navy Knox, whereby all acquisitions of real estate of every character and all leases would be submitted to the Naval Affairs Committees of the Senate and of the House of Representatives." U.S., Congressional Record, 82d Cong., 1st Sess., 1951, XCVII, Part 4, 5435.

was finally formalized as an important part of the 1944 statutory requirement.

Particular real estate transactions of the armed services were further subjected to prior committee approval by a 1949 statute.[10] This statute authorized the Secretary of the Air Force, or either secretary of the other two military departments when so directed by the Secretary of Defense, to acquire lands for, or the rights to the use of lands as, proving grounds for guided missiles and other weapons. Before any particular decision under this authority could become effective, however, the Secretary of the Air Force had to obtain the approval of the committees on armed services. Section two stated:

> Prior to the acquisition under the authority of this section of any lands or rights or other interests pertaining thereto, the Secretary of the Air Force shall come into agreement with the Armed Services Committee of the Senate and the House of Representatives with respect to the acquisition of such lands, rights, or other interests.[11]

This reservation of approval to the two congressional committees, interestingly enough, enabled the armed services committees to take part in international affairs and foreign relations that are generally assumed to be the sole function of the President and the Senate. The requirement of review and clearance, according to the conference report accompanying the bill, applied to all

---

10. U.S., *Statutes at Large*, LXIII, Part 1, 66. The Senate Committee on Armed Services, during committee consideration of H.R. 1741, inserted the requirement in the bill. See U.S., Congress, Senate, 81st Cong., 1st Sess., 1949, Senate Report 216 to accompany H.R. 1741.

11. U.S., *Statutes at Large*, loc. cit.

international agreements and treaties involving the acquisition of rights, in foreign countries, to the use of lands as missile testing grounds and ranges. The report declared:

> The Senate amendment is applicable not only to the acquisition of lands or rights or other interests pertaining thereto located within the United States but also to the acquisition of any lands or rights or other interests pertaining thereto through any type of agreement or treaty with any foreign nation.[12]

The Secretary of the Air Force took the position that executive agreements to acquire the use of lands in foreign nations for this purpose could not be subjected to committee control. The office of the Secretary continued to honor the requirement, however, in order to prevent controversy between the Air Force Department and the armed services committees.[13]

The next instance of formal committee clearance is Public Law 155,[14] a construction authorization statute for the three military departments, which was enacted in 1951. This Act not only dealt with the real estate activities of the armed services, but also imposed prior committee approval upon activities of the Federal Civil Defense Administration. Section 601 of Title VI[15] de-

---

12. Conference Committee Report to accompany H.R. 1741, U.S., Congressional Record, 81st Cong., 1st Sess., 1949, XCV, Part 4, 5610.

13. Interview with Mr. John A. Johnson, general counsel, Department of the Air Force, January 8, 1957.

14. U.S., Statutes at Large, LXV, 336.

15. Ibid., p. 365.

clared that these agencies had to "come into agreement with the Committee on Armed Services of the Senate and of the House of Representatives with respect to those real estate actions . . . "[16] involving an estimated value in excess of $25,000. The definition of real estate actions was very broad. It included: (1) acquisition of real property by sale or lease, (2) leasing of government-owned real property, (3) transfer of property between the military departments or such departments and other federal agencies or a military department and a state, and (4) reports, to a disposal agency, of excess government-owned real property.

The insertion into a statute authorizing military construction of a general proviso requiring committee clearance came at the end of a conflict between the President and Congress. An earlier bill[17] containing a similar requirement had been vetoed by President Truman in the same session. Truman vetoed this bill because he thought that the committee clearance procedure would lead to inefficiency and would impose unnecessary additional burdens upon the executive branch in the administration of the real estate program. The clearance requirement would, according to the President's veto message, necessitate reporting almost all real estate actions of the executive agencies named and would thus not only result in a serious delay in the execution of such transactions, but also would uneconomically centralize the approval of transactions previously consummated in the field.[18]

---

16. Ibid.

17. See H.R. 3096, U.S., Congressional Record, 82d Cong., 1st Sess., 1951, XCVII, Part 3, 4190.

18. Only one short paragraph of the veto message touched upon the constitutionality of the approval procedure. Pres-

14

The President vetoed the bill on May 15, 1951. The House of Representatives entered upon a full-scale debate of the bill and the President's action immediately and repassed the bill over the presidential veto just two days later.[19] The Senate failed to act on the vetoed bill. However, when H.R. 4914 (which later became Public Law 155) was before the House Committee On Armed Services later in the session, the Committee took advantage of the situation to insert the previously vetoed requirement of committee approval into the construction bill as a general proviso.[20] After further minor amendments by the Senate Committee on Armed Services and consideration by the conference committee established to eliminate the differences in the two versions of the bill, the committee approval requirement--Section 601-- was included in the bill.[21]

The conference report, containing the bill worked out by

---

ident Truman declared: "Finally, I am concerned by what appears to me to be a gradual trend on the part of the legislative branch to participate to an even greater extent in the actual execution and administration of the laws. Under our system of government it is contemplated that the Congress will enact the laws and will leave their administration and execution to the executive branch. The delays discussed above, which would inhere in the enactment of H.R. 3096, testify to the wisdom of that constitutional policy." U.S., Congressional Record, 82d Cong., 1st Sess., 1951, XCVII, Part 4, p. 5375.

19. Ibid., pp. 5444-5445.

20. U.S., Congress, House, Committee on Armed Services, 82d Cong., 1st Sess., 1951, House Report 767 to accompany H.R. 4914, p. 20.

21. See U.S., Congress, Conference Committee, House Report 974 to accompany H.R. 4914, Congressional Record, 82d Cong., 1st Sess., 1951, XCVII, Part 9, 11531.

the conference committee, was not issued until September 14, 1951. It was accepted by both chambers the same day with little debate. [22] Because of the passage of the bill late in the session and the need for some sort of statute authorizing continued military construction during the Korean emergency, President Truman had no choice but to approve the bill. This presidential approval established the statutory basis for committee clearance of a large number of real estate transactions of the military departments and the Federal Civil Defense Administration; it is still operative.

The same statute which contained the controversial Section 601 included a practically unnoticed earlier section which also established a requirement of committee approval. [23] This requirement was attached to a fifty-million dollar authorization for Army depot facilities in the continental United States. It was much broader in nature than the later general proviso. It required all real estate transactions and all proposed construction activities relating to the specified facilities to be reviewed and approved by the armed services committees of both chambers. None of the evidence available helps to explain why the Army depot facilities were singled out for this special requirement.

In the military construction bill passed in 1952, the military departments were once again directed to follow the procedure of committee clearance. [24] This bill authorized the secretaries of the departments, under the direction of the Secretary of Defense, [25] to use a general lump-

---

22. Ibid., pp. 11531, 11362.

23. U.S., Statutes at Large, LXV, 342.

24. U.S., Statutes at Large, LXVI, 606.

25. See Sections 102, 202, and 302 of the statute. Ibid., pp. 609, 613, and 622 respectively.

16

sum grant of funds to establish and develop classified military installations. The real estate transactions and the construction costs involving the expenditure of such funds, however, could become effective only after the departmental secretary had "come into agreement" with the armed services committees.

Prior committee approval requirements in all these cases applied to administrative decisions of the regular military departments. In two instances in recent years the Department of Defense itself has also been directed to follow the clearance procedure. In these two cases, however, the final approval had to be obtained from the appropriations committees, rather than the armed services committees. The first of these occurred in 1953 when the Supplemental Appropriation Act for fiscal year 1954[26] was passed. Section 805 of Chapter VIII granted the Defense Department a certain amount of latitude in use of any unspent funds appropriated in earlier Acts for specified defense purposes; such funds could be expended for public works projects authorized during the first session of the Eighty-third Congress. Before any such transfers of funds could take place, however, the department was required to clear each decision with the committees on appropriations.[27]

This particular provision was included in the bill because the appropriations committees did not have time to carry out a detailed review of the requests of the military departments. These requests for additional funds were submitted late in the first session of the Eighty-third Congress. Rather than appropriate additional funds, Congress authorized a general transfer, among the various programs of the military departments, of funds already available. The requirement of prior com-

---

26. U.S., Statutes at Large, LXVII, 418.

27. Ibid., p. 429.

mittee approval served as a convenient device to control this rather broad discretionary authority which became necessary if no new appropriations were to be granted.

The second instance of the appropriation committees' supervision of the activities of the Defense Department is found in a proviso inserted in the Department of Defense Appropriation Act for fiscal year 1956.[28] The requirement of committee approval was contained in Section 638. Under this proviso, the department had to obtain committee approval before it could make use of funds appropriated for the discontinuance and disposal of any government-owned manufacturing or commercial facilities providing supplies and services for the support of the nation's military establishment, e.g., the Rope-walk at the Boston naval shipyard, paint manufacturing plants operated by the Navy, and printing plants for recruitment publicity.

The proviso was first inserted into the appropriations bill by the House Committee on Appropriations. The reason for this action can be traced to the Committee's concern about the possible consequences of a policy announced earlier in the year by the executive branch. Both the Bureau of the Budget and the Defense Department had issued official directives to the effect that industrial and commercial facilities owned and operated by the government were to be discontinued if the products and services could be obtained from private business firms.[29] This was part of the general movement underway in the executive branch to eliminate all unnecessary government competition with private business. The House Committee believed that, in many cases, the discontinuance and disposal of such facilities might

---

28. Public Law 157 (1955).

29. See Bureau of the Budget Bulletin No. 55-4, January 15, 1955, and Department of Defense Directive No. 4100.15, February 8, 1955, as reissued April 27, 1955.

"result in a loss of trained personnel and know-how within the departments with the dispersal of tools and facilities and result in an actually greater cost to the Government over a period of years."[30]

In order to assure some sort of legislative supervision over the applications of the policy of the executive branch, the House Committee on Appropriations, therefore, inserted the committee clearance requirement into the bill. The proviso was accepted by the lower chamber, and after slight amendment by the Senate Committee on Appropriations and rewording in the conference committee, it was included in the bill as Section 638. The requirement read:

> No part of the funds appropriated in this Act may be used for the disposal or transfer by contract or otherwise of work that has been for a period of three years or more performed by civilian personnel of the Department of Defense unless justified to the Appropriations Committees of the Senate and House of Representatives, at least ninety days in advance of such disposal or transfer, that its discontinuance is economically sound and the work is capable of performance by a contractor without danger to the national security: Provided, That no such disposal or transfer shall be made if disapproved by either committee within the ninety-day period by written notice to the Secretary of Defense.[31]

President Eisenhower was openly opposed to this particular provision, but he signed the bill because the funds provided by it were urgently needed for the continued

---

30. U.S., Congress, House, 84th Cong., 1st Sess., 1955, House Report 493 to accompany H.R. 6042, p. 14.

31. Section 638 of Public Law 155.

operation of the military departments. His signature was accompanied by a message announcing his opposition to Section 638. The President declared that the requirement was an unconstitutional invasion of the functions of the executive branch. According to the President's message, it allowed Congress to participate in the administration of a statute in a way contrary to the constitutional rule of the separation-of-powers. President Eisenhower also served notice on Congress that the committee clearance proviso would be "regarded as invalid by the executive branch of the Government in the administration of H.R. 6042 unless otherwise determined by a court of competent jurisdiction."[32]

In the light of the succeeding events, however, it seems that this presidential challenge went unheard. On August 8, 1955, the Department of Defense proceeded to submit fourteen proposed disposals to the Committees on Appropriations. The Senate committee reviewed these decisions immediately and temporarily disapproved only one of them. The House committee requested that the Defense Department postpone any disposal until the committee could meet and review the proposals in detail. The department notified the committee on November 3, 1955, that it would hold up any action on the disposals for ninety days.[33] This postponement allowed the House

---

32. U.S., Congressional Record, 84th Cong., 1st Sess., 1955, CI, No. 118, 8997. Attorney General Brownell wrote an opinion which concluded that the disapproval of such decisions by a committee of Congress was unconstitutional. See Advance (slip) Opinions, Opinions of the Attorneys General of the United States, July 13, 1955.

33. See Kofmehl, op. cit., supra, Chapter One, n. 2, pp. 222-223, n. 37. The Defense Department may have been prompted to accept this request because of a decision by the Comptroller General. On August 20, 1955, Representative Porter Hardy announced that he had received a

20

committee to begin its review of the proposals immediately after the start of the second session of the Eighty-fourth Congress. Furthermore, the Defense Department continued to honor the requirement during the entire second session, during which time it submitted a total of 112 proposed disposals to the committees.[34]

The requirement of committee clearance was not renewed in the 1957 Defense Department Appropriation Act. The House Committee on Appropriations included it in the Defense Appropriation bill for 1957 as Section 633, but when the bill came up for action by the House of Representatives, the House did not go along with its appropriations committee and eliminated this section of the bill.[35] The successful opposition to the proviso was led by the proponents of a reduction in government competition with private business who viewed committee review as an unnecessary delay in the disposal of competitive government facilities operated by the Department of Defense.

The use of committee clearance has not been limited to the activities of the Department of Defense and the military departments. Congress has also found this device useful as a means for supervising and controlling the use of discretionary authority entrusted to other executive agencies. In 1954, for example, Congress relied upon the committee oversight procedure to control the

written notification from the Comptroller General that any expenditures made by the Defense Department under Public Law 155 in violation of Section 638 would be disallowed by the General Accounting Office. Ibid.

34. Letter from Mr. Everard H. Smith, chief clerk, Senate Committee on Appropriations, February 9, 1957.

35. Statement by Representative Vinson in U.S., Congressional Record, 84th Cong., 2d Sess., 1955, CII, No. 125, 12606.

broad discretion delegated to the Administrator of General Services and the Postmaster General in the "Public Buildings Purchase Contract Act of 1954."[36] This statute established a new system for the acquisition of additional space needed for the activities of the national government. It amended the Public Buildings Act of 1949 by adding a new authorization which allowed both the Administrator of General Services and the Postmaster General to enter into lease-purchase contracts for the construction of the necessary buildings.[37] Such contracts could be entered into with any person, partnership, corporation, or other private or public entity. The contracting party would then build the required building and lease it to the national government. The annual payments for the lease would be applied against a determined total purchase price and, at the end of a stated period, the national government would acquire ownership of the building.

The delegated discretion of both the Administrator of General Services and the Postmaster General was limited by only two general statutory standards. The two executive offices were authorized to enter into lease-purchase contracts if they found, first, that the needed space could not be found in government buildings in the area and, second, that the best interests of the United States would be served by such contracts. The specific use of this authority was circumscribed, however, by the requirement that each proposed contract had to be approved by resolutions of the congressional committees

36. U.S., Statutes at Large, LXVIII, Part 1, 518.

37. Contracts to meet the general space requirements of the national government were under the jurisdiction of the former officer. The Postmaster General was granted authority to enter into such contracts only for meeting the requirements for additional space relating to postal activities.

on public works.[38] For example, Section 411(e), which concerned the Administrator of General Services, declared:

> No appropriations shall be made for purchase contract projects which have not been approved by resolutions adopted by the Committees on Public Works of the Senate and House of Representatives, within three years after the date of enactment of this Act.[39]

The specific language of this requirement was significant. As can be seen, the section was carefully written in such a way as to tie the committee approval requirement directly to the congressional power of appropriation. This represented the climax of a "war of words" between Congress and the Eisenhower administration. The statutory clearance requirements passed in previous administrations had made no specific mention of the congressional appropriation power. They simply declared that the department or agency involved had to "come into agreement" with specified committees. This same language was copied by the Senate Committee on Public Works in 1954 when it inserted a committee clearance proviso in the lease-purchase bill. The committee amendment, which was accepted by the Senate, simply stated that the Administrator of General Services had to "come into agreement" with the public works committees in regard to proposed contracts involving a certain minimum amount of money.[40]

---

38. U.S., Statutes at Large, LXVIII, Part 1, 519 and 521. Each contract had to be approved by the Director of the Bureau of the Budget by a written statement that "the execution of such agreement is necessary and is in conformity with the policy of the President." Ibid., p. 519.

39. The discretion delegated to the Postmaster General was limited by a similar proviso. See Ibid., p. 522.

The executive branch strongly opposed this language. In the eyes of the President and his advisors, the language implied that the legislative body had an inherent constitutional power to require committee clearance of administrative decisions. According to the Eisenhower administration, the Constitution gave no such general power to Congress. However, the executive branch was willing to concede that Congress could attach such a condition to congressional appropriations. It thus agreed that the committee approval requirement would be acceptable if the language clearly and specifically connected it to the appropriation power.

The members of the conference committee formed to work out the differences in the House and Senate versions of the lease-purchase bill were willing to accept this compromise. They thus eliminated the Senate language and inserted the language which tied the clearance directive specifically to the appropriation power. [41]

The outcome of this conflict was a Pyrrhic victory for the executive branch. It did not in any way eliminate committee control over administrative decisions in the immediate case, and, more importantly, it established a precedent which Congress could use in later instances when it wanted to set up a committee oversight procedure. Congress could simply copy the language accepted by the administration in this case. As we shall see below, Congress has taken advantage of this pre-

40. U.S., Congress, Senate, Committee on Public Works, 83d Cong., 2d Sess., 1954, Senate Report 1084 to accompany H.R. 6342, pp. 3-4.

41. U.S., Congress, Conference Committee, 83d Cong., 2d Sess., 1954, House Report 1923 to accompany H.R. 6342, pp. 5-6.

cedent to establish committee clearance in later instances.

The public works committees continued to engage in the clearance of lease-purchase contracts for about three years. On July 22, 1957, however, the requirement of prior committee approval expired along with the entire lease-purchase program. The first and second sessions of the 85th Congress adjourned without renewing this program.[42] The clearance activities of these committees have thus evidently come to an end.

The Department of Agriculture is another executive agency that has recently been required to follow the committee clearance procedure. This requirement was imposed on the department in the Watershed Protection and Flood Prevention Act of 1954.[43] This statute authorized the Secretary of Agriculture to assist local soil and water conservation districts in planning and building small structures on tributary streams in order to prevent periodic flooding of farmlands and to promote soil conservation. The responsibility for the initiation of such projects,[44] and their actual construction rested with the local organizations, but the Secretary of Agriculture was empowered to cooperate in studies and plans for such projects. Furthermore, the Secretary was also authorized to enter into agreements with these organizations to furnish federal financial assistance if he found the proposed watershed project financially feasible.

---

42. See Congressional Quarterly Almanac, Vol. XIII, 1957, p. 684, and Congressional Quarterly Weekly Report, Vol. XVI, No. 35, 1958, p. 1142.

43. U.S., Statutes at Large, LXVIII, Part 1, 666.

44. No project under this statute could exceed 250,000 acres nor include any single structure that provided more than 5,000 acre-feet of total capacity.

In the case of certain decisions pursuant to this discretionary authority, the Secretary was directed to obtain prior approval of the House Committee on Agriculture and the Senate Committee on Agriculture and Forestry. The statutory requirement, based again on the congressional power of appropriation, stated that no appropriations could be granted for any proposed plan of assistance including any single structure providing more than 2,500 acre-feet of total capacity unless each committee passed a resolution approving such a plan.[45]

This procedure was in effect for only one session of Congress. It was amended in the second session of the 84th Congress by the enactment of Public Law 1018. The new statute divided the jurisdiction for committee review and approval between the Agriculture Committees and the Public Works Committees of Congress. According to the terms of the statute, the Committees on Agriculture were to review all future proposed projects involving more than a $250,000 federal contribution or including any structure between 2,500 and 4,000 acre-feet of the total capacity of the watershed project. If the project were to include any structure that provided more than 4,000 acre-feet of the total capacity, however, approval had to be obtained from the Public Works Committees.[46]

This division of the clearance function between the two sets of committees resulted from a compromise worked out by the conference committee established to settle the differences in the Senate and House versions of the bill that was to become Public Law 1018. The House version had assigned the function completely to the Agriculture Committees, as in the earlier 1954 statute. When the

---

45. U.S., Statutes at Large, loc. cit.

46. Public Law 1018 (1956), p. 1.

26

bill came to the Senate, however, it was assigned to the Senate Committee on Public Works rather than the Agriculture Committee. This Committee, perhaps as a result of concern about the possible interference of the small stream projects with the work of the Army Corps of Engineers, amended the bill to read that the proposed decisions of the Department of Agriculture had to be reviewed and approved by the Public Works Committees. The upper chamber passed the bill with this proviso. In order to eliminate the deadlock between the committees, the conference committee finally arrived at the solution of the divided clearance function.[47]

One further recent example of committee oversight is contained in the Small Reclamation Projects Act of 1956.[48] The purpose of this statute was to establish a system for assisting soil and water conservation districts in the seventeen reclamation states of the West in developing water-storage projects. The Secretary of the Interior was authorized to assist in the construction of such projects by loaning or granting funds to the local organizations. He was directed to negotiate, and enter into a contract of assistance with, any qualified district organization desiring to obtain federal aid for the construction of a small project.

According to the terms of the statute, the Secretary, could not proceed to execute any such contract until sixty days after it had been submitted to Congress for consideration by the Committees on Interior and Insular Affairs.[49] Either committee could nullify any proposed

47. See U.S., Congressional Record, 84th Cong., 2d Sess., 1956, CII, No. 66, 12429.

48. Public Law 984 (1956).

49. The statute did not specify any particular committees, but only that the contracts were to be considered by the "ap-

contract during this laying period by adopting a formal resolution of disapproval. The Interior Department, in such a case, could not proceed to execute the contract unless it was specifically approved by a regular act of Congress. The statute read that "in the event either committee disapproves the project proposal, the Secretary shall not proceed further unless the Congress has approved the same."[50]

President Eisenhower once again challenged the authority of Congress to include such a general approval requirement in a statute. Although he signed the bill, the President declared that he would have withheld his signature if Congress had been in session; he alleged "constitutional defects" in the proviso establishing committee clearance of the contracts entered into by the Secretary of the Interior, and went on to say:

> Because of the general merit of this measure, I am approving it. The Secretary of the Interior will review project proposals received by the Department and will prepare to take action as soon

propriate committees." Ibid., Section 4(c). Such activities of the Interior Department, however, would of course come under the jurisdiction of the interior committees.

50. Ibid. This latter addition to the committee clearance requirement regarding statutory approval of a disapproved contract seems entirely redundant when viewed either as a safeguard against the Secretary of the Interior disregarding committee nullification or as a grant of authority to the President and Congress to approve a contract by a regular legislative act. In the former case the statute specifically prohibits the Secretary from executing a contract that has been rejected by either committee. As far as the latter case is concerned, it would seem that even in the absence of a statutory grant the President and the Congress have plenary power to override a decision of a committee of the legislative body by a regular statute. A statutory grant of such power seems entirely unnecessary.

as appropriations are made to implement the bill and section 4(c) [the review procedure section] has been removed or revised. If the Congress will act promptly after it convenes in January, there need be no delay in starting this program.[51]

On January 7, 1957, Representative Engle introduced H.R. 2146 amending this section in the Small Reclamation Projects Act of 1956. The bill changed the languages in such a manner as to establish a specific connection between the clearance requirement and the appropriation power. It declared that appropriations could be made for any project only if the project were not specifically disapproved by a resolution of either committee on interior and insular affairs. It also deleted the requirement of congressional approval for the execution of projects nullified by the reviewing committees. The House Committee on Interior and Insular Affairs reviewed this bill and, after rewording it slightly, reported it favorably to the House.[52] The committee amendment, in turn, was reworded during the consideration of the bill on the floor of the House and was then passed by the lower chamber.[53] The final House version thus read:

No appropriation shall be made for financial participation in any such project prior to 60 calendar days (which 60 days, however, shall not include days on which either the House of Representatives or the Senate is not in session because

51. Quoted in "Accomplishments of the House Committee on Interior and Insular Affairs During the 84th Congress," Committee Print No. 18, September 1, 1956, p. 9.

52. U.S., Congress, House, Committee on Interior and Insular Affairs, 85th Cong., 1st Sess., 1957, House Report 25 to accompany H.R. 2146, p. 1.

53. U.S., Congressional Record, 85th Cong., 1st Sess., 1957, CIII, No. 64, 4931.

of an adjournment of more than 3 calendar days to a day certain) from the date on which the Secretary's findings and approval are submitted to the Congress and then only if, within said 60 days, neither the House nor the Senate Interior and Insular Affairs Committee disapproves the project proposal by committee resolution.[54]

The House bill was sent to the Senate and referred to the Senate Committee on Interior and Insular Affairs. It was favorably reported by this committee without amendment,[55] and promptly accepted by the upper house. The Bureau of the Budget, speaking for the executive branch, favored a requirement simply calling for the submittal to Congress of periodic reports concerning the administration of the program, rather than any sort of committee approval proviso.[56] However, faced as it was with language that had been accepted in the 1954 lease-purchase statute and the 1954 Watershed Construction Act, the Bureau had no real choice but to recommend presidential approval. The President signed the bill

---

54. Ibid. The new language connecting the committee clearance requirement to the congressional appropriation power was based on similar language found in the earlier lease-purchase contract statute of 1954 and the Watershed Protection & Flood Prevention Act of 1954. According to Representative Engle, the sponsor of the amendment, the language of the earlier statutes and acceptance of such language by the White House served as the precedent for the amendment. See Ibid., p. 4929.

55. See U.S., Congress, Senate, 85th Cong., 1st Sess., May 8, 1957, Senate Report 216 to accompany H.R. 2146.

56. See the letter from Percival Brundage, Director, Bureau of the Budget, to Senator James E. Murray, Chairman of the Senate Committee on Interior and Insular Affairs, dated March 5, 1957, in U.S. Code Congressional and Administrative News, Volume 2 (1957), p. 1203.

and it became Public Law 47. The Small Reclamation Project Act of 1956, as amended by the addition of a new Section 4(d) in place of the earlier Section 4(c), thus provides the statutory basis for one of the instances of committee clearance that is presently in operation.

An interesting variation from the normal committee clearance pattern is found in the final instance to be mentioned. In this case the function of review and clearance of administrative decisions was granted to the chairman of a single committee of the lower house. The requirement was first established in the Supplemental Appropriations Act for fiscal year 1953;[57] this was the first time that the clearance function was delegated to the chairman of a committee rather than to a related committee in each legislative chamber. Section 1413 of the 1952 statute stated that the Director of the Bureau of the Budget could change or amend Bureau of the Budget Circular A-45 only with the approval of the chairman of the House Committee on Appropriations.[58]

The Budget circular that was the object of control in this particular case established criteria and general procedural requirements that were to be followed by agencies of the national government in setting and administering rents and service charges for quarters furnished by such agencies to their employees.[59] The requirement of approval by the chairman of the house appropriations committee was intended to insure legislative control over the general scheme for determining the

---

57. U.S., Statutes at Large, LXVI, 637.

58. Ibid., p. 661.

59. See Bureau of the Budget Circular No. A-45, July 9, 1951, and Bureau of the Budget Circular No. A-45 (revised), June 3, 1952.

31

rent charged government employees living in housing furnished by the national government. This method of review and clearance of the decisions of the Director of the Bureau of the Budget regarding the amendment or modification of Bureau of the Budget Circular A-45 has been reestablished in each successive year since it first appeared in 1952.[60] It has thus become a fairly well established practice and represents a unique variation from the normal pattern of clearance by committees.

---

60. See U.S., Statutes at Large, LXVII, 418, Section 1312; U.S., Statutes at Large, LXVII, Part 1, 829, Section 1309; Public Law 110 (1955), Section 208; Public Law 578 (1956), Section 208; Public Law 85-48, Section 208 (1957).

III
INFORMAL COMMITTEE CLEARANCE

The first instance of informal committee clearance to be reported concerns the review and approval by the Joint Committee on Internal Revenue Taxation of certain Internal Revenue Service tax refunds. This example is quite significant in two respects. First, it is apparently the only case involving clearance by a joint committee of Congress. Secondly, this is the earliest known instance of committee clearance. The practice, which is still in operation, developed during the latter years of the second decade of this century, thus making its appearance on the national government scene quite some

61. The following instances of committee oversight were obtained from personal interviews with members of the professional staffs of congressional committees and officers in several of the executive departments in Washington, D. C. This chapter could not have been included without the cooperation of these persons, who gave so freely of their time and information.

time before any of the other instances of formal or informal clearance.

This committee oversight arrangement grew out of a "prior reporting" requirement regarding particular tax refunds of the Bureau of Internal Revenue contained in the Urgent Deficiency Act of 1927.[62] The statutory stipulation directed the Bureau to report all tax refunds involving more than $75,000 to the Joint Committee on Internal Revenue Taxation sixty days before they were actually paid. Although the statutory language did not explicitly grant a veto power to the joint committee, an arrangement soon developed whereby only the committee-approved decisions would be carried out.[63]

This early understanding has continued as the unwritten interpretation of the "prior reporting" requirement found in all later statutes concerning tax refunds. At the present time, the Internal Revenue Service thus submits each proposed tax credit exceeding $100,000 to the joint committee thirty days before it is to be paid.[64] If it meets with the approval of the committee, it is validated and can then be paid. If, on the other hand, the joint committee objects to a particular refund, it is not made at all or it is revised in order to satisfy the committee's objections before payment. As Kofmehl reports, "a refund or credit to which the Joint Tax Committee ob-

---

62. U.S., Statutes at Large, XLIV, Part 2, 1250. This requirement was established at this time, according to Mr. Colin Stam, chief of staff of the joint committee, as a result of objections in Congress to the continual large tax refunds that had first begun shortly after World War I. Interview with Mr. Colin Stam, chief of staff, Joint Committee on Internal Revenue Taxation, January 10, 1957.

63. Ibid.

64. See Subtitle F, Chapter 65, Subchapter A, Section 6405(a) of U.S., Statutes at Large, LXVIII(A), 792.

jected was not likely to be made unless the taxpayer concerned sued and won."[65]

Some of the activities of the military departments and the Department of Defense in the construction field have been subject to informal control by the armed services committees of Congress. Such an informal arrangement was, for example, established to supervise the military departments' use of emergency funds that were authorized by a 1951 construction authorization statute.[66] This statute authorized a lump-sum grant of funds for the military departments to be used "for restoration or replacement of facilities damaged or destroyed . . .,"[67] or for other urgent construction needs not covered in the regular appropriation items. Although the statute did not specifically require the military departments to obtain the approval of the armed services committees before any of the funds were used, the departments have consistently cleared with the committees. The use by the military departments of emergency funds authorized by subsequent statutes have similarly been subject to this informal arrangement. In practice, the military departments must submit each proposed decision to use emergency funds to both armed services committees for review and approval.

---

65. Kofmehl, op. cit., supra, Chapter I, n. 2, p. 206. This was a reported statement of Dr. Roy Blough, formerly director of tax research and assistant to the Secretary of the Treasury.

66. U.S., Statutes at Large, LXV, 336. This is Public Law 155, the Military Public Works Act, that was passed in the first session of the Eighty-second Congress. It is the same act that established the general statutory requirement of committee approval of real-estate transactions of the military departments and the Federal Civil Defense Administration involving $25,000 or more. See supra, Chapter Two, p.

67. Ibid., p. 342.

The Department of the Air Force, for example, submitted in 1953 a proposed decision to use 2.9 million dollars of the emergency fund established by the 1951 statute to restore and replace, at Warner Robins (Georgia) Air Force Base, facilities which had been destroyed by a tornado earlier in the year.[68] The Army Department similarly proposed to spend $199,000 of an authorized emergency fund in 1955 to replace an officers' mess hall that had burned the previous year; the proposal was also submitted to the armed services committees for clearance.[69] A more recent example of this informal procedure involved a proposal of the Department of the Navy submitted to the committees in February, 1957. This proposal concerned a contemplated decision to spend $26,000 of an emergency fund to replace a water-treatment plant laboratory on Guam that had been destroyed by an explosion in November, 1956.[70]

68. U.S., Congress, House, Committee on Armed Services, 83d Cong., 1st Sess., 1953, Armed Services Paper No. 20, p. 840. These armed services papers are published miscellaneous hearings on bills, resolutions, and other legislative matters conducted by the House Committee on Armed Services and its subcommittees. They are paged continuously for binding at the end of each session of Congress under the title "Hearings before Committee on Armed services of the House of Representatives on Sundry Legislation Affecting the Naval and Military Establishments." Further citation of this source will be by initial, "A.S.P." None of the activities of the Senate Committee on Armed Services relating to review of these decisions-- or, for that matter, any other decisions that are submitted to the committees under either a formal or an informal procedure--are reported in published form.

69. U.S., Congress, House, Committee on Armed Services, 84th Cong., 1st Sess., 1955, A.S.P. 31, p. 4416.

70. U.S., Congress, House, Committee on Armed Services, 85th Cong., 1st Sess., 1957, A.S.P. No. 12, p. 393. Other examples, among many, can be found in: U.S.,

Public Law 968, a military construction bill enacted in the second session of the Eighty-fourth Congress, gave occasion for informal committee control over Defense Department decisions. This statute served as a substitute for a military construction bill that had been passed by Congress earlier in the session and vetoed by President Eisenhower. The vetoed bill, H.R. 9893, included a general authorization for the Secretary of Defense to enter into contracts with private contractors for the construction or acquisition of so-called Capehart housing to provide living quarters for the military and civilian personnel of the armed services stationed at various locations. Under this bill, however, no such contract could become effective until the Secretary of Defense had come "into agreement with the Armed Services Committees of the Senate and House of Representatives."[71]

President Eisenhower vetoed this bill when it was submitted to him for the necessary presidential approval. The veto was based upon the requirement of committee review and approval contained in the statute. The Pres-

---

Congress, House, Committee on Armed Services, 83d Cong., 2d Sess., 1954, A.S.P. No. 70, p. 3819; U.S., Congress, House, Committee on Armed Services, 84th Cong., 1st Sess., 1955, A.S.P. No. 8, p. 884; and U.S., Congress, House, Committee on Armed Services, 85th Cong., 1st Sess., 1957, No. 20, p. 547.

71. Quoted in U.S., Congress, Senate, Committee on Armed Services, 84th Cong., 2d Sess., Senate Report 2775 to accompany H.R. 12270, p. 5. Section 301 of H.R. 9893, the vetoed bill, also required the Secretary of Defense to "come into agreement" with the committees concerning the utilization of an appropriation authorization totaling approximately $16,000,000 for the construction of Talos (guided missile) site facilities. U.S., Congress, Conference Committee, 84th Cong., 2d Sess., 1956, House Report 2641 to accompany H.R. 9893, p. 15.

ident, in his veto message, described such a requirement as a "serious departure from the separation of
powers as provided by the Constitution."[72]

The House Committee on Armed Services met on the day
after the veto message to draw up a new bill. The committee simply removed the objectionable requirement of
committee approval in the vetoed bill and reintroduced
the bill as H.R. 12270. It passed the House of Representatives and was sent to the Senate for the necessary
concurrence.[73] When the bill was before the Senate
Committee on Armed Services, however, the Committee
added a new requirement which became Section 419 of
Public Law 968. Although this proviso did not empower
the armed services committees to nullify any contract
that was entered into by the Secretary of Defense to provide the needed housing, it did declare that no such
contract could become effective until 180 days after it
had been submitted to the Committees on Armed Services
or until both committees stated in writing that they had
no further questions concerning the proposed contract.[74]

The report of the Senate Committee on Armed Services
that accompanied the bill to the floor of the Senate
declared that "the committee has again inserted language
in the bill to insure that the armed services committees
retain adequate supervision over the construction or
acquisition of military housing units."[75] It also stated
that, although the new language did not involve a "coming

---

72. U.S., Congressional Record, 84th Cong., 2d Sess., 1956,
CII, No. 120, 11788.

73. U.S., Congressional Record, 84th Cong., 2d Sess., 1956,
CII, No. 121, 11933.

74. Section 419(2) of Public Law 968 (1956).

75. Senate Report 2775, supra, n. 71.

into agreement" requirement, "it does provide for the submission of timely reports by the Secretary of Defense which, if properly submitted, will provide Congress with a basis for proper legislative review as well as any further legislative action that may be found to be necessary."[76]

The practical effect of this prior reporting requirement, however, when coupled with the extended laying period of six months, actually eliminated the necessity of any legislative action on the part of Congress to control the use of the authority delegated to the Secretary of Defense. In spite of the cautious statutory language, the actual result of the requirement was to place the power of approval and disapproval of the proposed construction contracts in the armed services committees of Congress. This occurred because the Defense Department generally desired to begin construction on the necessary housing units as quickly as possible and did not want to postpone such construction for six months while the proposed contract remained before the committees. This laying period, according to the statute, could be waived only by the armed services committees. If these committees had any objections to particular items in the contract, therefore, the Department of Defense had to accept such criticisms and modify the contract to meet the objections of the committees and obtain a waiver of the remainder of the laying period. A refusal by the Department of Defense to follow such committee suggestions generally meant a six-month delay in the beginning of construction. In this fashion, the discretionary authority delegated to the Secretary of Defense by Congress became subject to committee review and clearance identical, for all practical purposes, to formal committee oversight.[77]

---

76. Ibid.

77. This interpretation was obtained from interviews with the

39

This practice persisted only a short while, however. In the next year, during its first session, the Eighty-fifth Congress eliminated the discretionary authority given to the Secretary of Defense. The Military Public Works Authorization Act[78] eliminated Section 419 of the earlier 1956 statute and stated specifically that after June 30, 1958, all family housing units to be acquired or constructed had to be authorized by annual military construction bills. The armed services committees were thus engaged in this particular form of prior committee approval for only about one year.

Another instance of informal clearance is associated with the negotiated disposals of surplus government property by the General Services Administration. The clearance function, in this case, has been carried out by the Committees on Government Operations. The requirement of prior committee approval was established by an agreement between GSA and the committees concerning the interpretation of a "prior reporting" proviso in a 1952 statute.

This statute[79] amended the Federal Property and Administrative Services Act of 1949 by extending until June 30,

---

following persons: Mr. Harry L. Wingate, Jr., chief clerk, Senate Armed Services Committee, January 7, 1957; Mr. John A. Johnson, general consel, Department of the Air Force, January 8, 1957; Major Watts, Office of Legislative Liaison, Department of the Army, January 8, 1957; Mr. Mansfield D. Sprague, general consel, Department of Defense, January 8, 1957. All of these interviewees agreed that the decisions of the Defense Department were actually subject to the final approval of the armed services committees.

78. Public Law 241 (1957). See also Congressional Quarterly Almanac, Volume XIII, 1957, pp. 683-684.

79. U.S., Statutes at Large, LXVI, 593.

1953, the authority of the Administrator of General Services to dispose of surplus property by negotiation rather than by advertised bidding. The statute also added a new proviso to this extension of statutory delegation of authority. The new requirement stated that "an explanatory statement shall be prepared and submitted to the appropriate committees of Congress and a copy preserved in the file of all cases where negotiated disposals occur."[80] This requirement, according to the Senate Committee on Government Operations, actually meant that such statements had to be submitted to the appropriate committees--the committees on government operations--prior to the actual disposal "in order that these committees may have up-to-date information on the extent of this program."[81]

The statutory language required only a report to the government operations committees before the GSA took any action, and it did not give specific authority to the committees to nullify a proposed negotiated disposal. An unwritten agreement was reached, however, between the GSA and the committees whereby only such proposed disposals as were acceptable to the committees would be carried out. The legal requirement of "prior reporting" thus became in actual practice the basis for another instance of committee clearance.[82]

---

80. Ibid.

81. U.S., Congress, Senate, Committee on Government Operations, 82d Cong., 2d Sess., 1952, Senate Report 2075 to accompany H.R. 5350, p. 5.

82. This "prior reporting" requirement has been carried over in the successive extensions of the disposal authority. See U.S., Statutes at Large, LXVII, 521; U.S., Statutes at Large, LXVIII, Part I, 474; Public Law 971 (1956); and Public Law 486 (1958). The particular understanding concerning the "prior requirement" directive accompanied the three earliest statutory extensions, according to Mr.

Some of the activities of the Department of the Interior have also been brought under the informal committee clearance procedure. This occurred on two separate occasions during the second session of the Eighty-fourth Congress. In both instances, interestingly enough, the requirement of committee review and approval was set up simply by an informal agreement entered into by the department and a committee of the House of Representatives. No Senate committee was involved in either informal agreement, nor was any committee of the upper house included in the clearance procedure established by the agreements. Both of these cases are rare examples of review of administrative decisions by a single committee of one chamber; as previously stated clearance by related House and Senate committees is more usual.

Secretary of the Interior Douglas McKay entered into an informal agreement with Chairman Bonner of the House Committee on Merchant Marine and Fisheries early in the second session of the Eighty-fourth Congress. This arrangement related to the national wildlife refuges under the jurisdiction of the Fish and Wildlife Service of the Department of the Interior. A long chain of events led up to this agreement. On March 29, 1955, during the first session of the Eighty-fourth Congress, Representative Metcalf, introduced a bill which declared that it was the policy of the United States Congress to preserve and maintain the areas of the national wildlife refuges. The bill then stated that the "Secretary of the Interior shall not dispose of, or relinquish any of the national wildlife refuges, or parts thereof, without the

Walter L. Reynolds, chief clerk and staff director, Senate Committee on Governments Operations, in an interview conducted on January 11, 1957. This understanding, so firmly entrenched by 1958, undoubtedly also accompanied the 1958 extension.

prior approval of Congress."[83] Metcalf introduced this bill because information had been brought to his attention that the Interior Department planned to begin allowing entry into the wildlife refuges for various purposes which, he alleged, would destroy the value of the refuges as sanctuaries for the nation's wildlife. He was especially concerned about the proposed leasing of portions of such areas to private companies for the purpose of petroleum exploration.

The House Committee on Merchant Marine and Fisheries was not able to hold hearing until early in the second session of the Eighty-fourth Congress. After the hearings, however, the bill was never reported out of the Committee. The House Committee recognized that special legislation to approve each decision of the Interior Department was impractical, but the members were unable to agree upon a satisfactory substitute method of congressional control.[84] In order to circumvent this stalemate and establish some sort of check upon the actions of the Department of Interior, Chairman Bonner wrote to Secretary McKay on March 21, 1956, requesting that the Interior Department consent to the following experimental procedure: whenever it was proposed to allow entry into the national wildlife refuges which would

---

83. Private copy of bill, H.R. 5306, obtained from Mr. John M. Drewry, chief counsel, House Committee on Merchant Marine and Fisheries. Representative Metcalf had no particular method of approval in mind. He stated that he would accept approval by a committee, a joint committee, or Congress as a whole. See "Wildlife Refuge Disposal Policy," Hearings before the Committee on Merchant Marine and Fisheries, House of Representatives, 84th Cong., 2d Sess., on H.R. 5306, January 19, 20, and February 20, 21, 1956, p. 8.

84. U.S., Congress, House, Committee on Merchant Marine and Fisheries, 84th Cong., 2d Sess., 1956, House Report, 1941, pursuant to H.R. 118, p. 11.

result in the relinquishment of the operating jurisdiction of the Fish and Wildlife Service, the Secretary would submit such proposal to the House Committee on Merchant Marine and Fisheries for review and clearance sixty days in advance of any contemplated action. The proposed decisions would then be carried out by the executive agency only if they were not disapproved by the House Committee. Secretary McKay agreed to such an arrangement and the informal clearance procedure, which is apparently still operative, was thus established.[85]

The second instance of single committee oversight, also involving the Interior Department, grew out of an agreement between the department and the House Committee on Interior and Insular Affairs. This agreement concerned the Interior Department's withdrawal or reservation from entrance, settlement, or sale, of public lands to be used by the military departments. It was brought about primarily because of the growing concern in the Western states about the large withdrawals, in those states, of public lands destined to become bombing and gunnery ranges, rocket and missile testing areas, and areas for teaching survival training. The Department of Defense in recent years, had asked the Interior Department to withdraw large parts of the public lands from entrance and settlement for the exclusive use of the military departments for such purposes. One application, for example, involved 2.8 million acres in the Black Rock Desert-Sahwave Mountain area in Northwest Nevada. Another application by the Defense Department requested that 1.2 million acres be withdrawn in the Saline-Panamint valley area of southeast central

---

85. Chairman Bonner's letter can be found ibid., p. 12. Secretary McKay's reply is printed ibid., p. 13.

California.[86] The Department of Defense, as of June 30, 1955, already owned or controlled fourteen million acres of land that had been withdrawn from the public domain. Applications for further withdrawals pending on that date totalled an additional eight million acres in the continental United States.[87] Since most of the public land area was located in the western part of the country, such large holdings and proposed future withdrawals became a serious matter in the eyes of the western states.

These increasingly large withdrawals of public lands finally prompted Representative Engle of California, chairman of the House Committee on Interior and Insular Affairs, to address a letter to Mr. Wesley A. D'Ewart, Assistant Secretary of the Interior for Land Management, during the recess between the first and second sessions of the Eighty-fourth Congress;[88] he asked that D'Ewart withhold his approval of any more applications for the withdrawal of public lands until the House Committee

---

86. "Accomplishments of the House Committee on Interior and Insular Affairs for the Eighty-fourth Congress." 84th Cong., 2d Sess., September 1, 1956, Committee Print No. 18, p. 41.

87. U.S., Congress, House, Committee on Interior and Insular Affairs, 84th Cong., 2d Sess., 1956, House Report 2856 to accompany H.R. 12185, p. 11.

88. The letters written by Engle and D'Ewart consummating this agreement are printed in "Withdrawal and Utilization of the Public Lands of the United States," Hearings before the Committee on Interior and Insular Affairs, House of Representatives, 84th Cong., 2d Sess. (Serial 29 - Defense Agencies), 1956, pp. 2-3. The popular descriptive title for this arrangement was obtained in a personal interview with Mr. George W. Abbott, committee counsel, House Committee on Interior and Insular Affairs, January 10, 1957.

could investigate the subject in the second session of the Eighty-fourth Congress. D'Ewart accepted this arrangement and thus agreed to establish what became popularly known in the Pentagon as the "Engle Freeze."

The House Committee on Interior and Insular Affairs held extensive hearings during the early months of the second session of the Eighty-fourth Congress. They extended from January to May, 1956.[89] The facts brought out in the hearings pointed to the conclusion that the Department of Defense had not created any effective system for supervising and reviewing the requests of the military departments for withdrawal of public lands. According to the committee, the evidence revealed that there was no centralized reporting system whereby the possibility of using lands already withdrawn by the different departments of the military establishment could be determined. Furthermore, the House committee was informed by Assistant Secretary D'Ewart that he found it virtually impossible to measure the requests for military uses of the public lands against the possible maximum utilization of the lands for other purposes. D'Ewart told the committee that "we are not in a position to weigh the economic impact of the withdrawal of substantial acreages against military necessity [sic.]."[90]

After these hearings, several bills were introduced in Congress to provide a congressional check upon public land withdrawals by the Interior Department. They required approval by an act of Congress of all withdrawals for defense purposes involving more than 5,000 acres.[91]

---

89. See "Withdrawals and Utilization of the Public Lands of the United States," supra, n. 88.

90. Ibid., p. 302.

91. See H.R. 10371, H.R. 10380, H.R. 10377, and H.R. 10367 of the 84th Cong., 2d Sess.

The bills were introduced late in the second session, however, and none were passed by the legislative body. In the meantime, an informal agreement was consummated between the Department of Interior and the House Committee on Interior and Insular Affairs in which the department agreed to submit all proposed withdrawals of public lands for the use of the military departments to the House committee for review and approval.[92]

This informal clearance arrangement continued in operation for over a year. It came to an end early in the second session of the Eighty-fifth Congress when President Eisenhower, on February 28, 1958, signed H.R. 5538.[93] This bill, like its unsuccessful 1956 predecessors, required statutory approval of public land withdrawals exceeding 5,000 acres. Since such withdrawals almost invariably involved more than 5,000 acres, this new statute had the effect of superseding review and approval by the House Committee on Interior and Insular Affairs.

Conclusion

Both formal and informal committee clearance have been used on many occasions to provide a mechanism of control of delegated bureaucratic discretion. These instances have appeared on the national government scene at various times during a period stretching from the late 1920's to the end of 1957, with the greater number of cases falling within the latter half of this period. The limited number of cases do not, of course, portend a wholesale substitution of this prior committee approval device for the older and more traditional methods of legislative surveillance and control. A close scrutiny,

---

92.   Interview with Mr. George W. Abbott, *supra*, n. 88.

93.   Public Law 337 (1958).

however, does lead to the conclusion that the lawmakers at the nation's capitol have found this device particularly useful under any one or some combination of three special circumstances.

The first such circumstance is a demand for especially close legislative supervision and control arising out of dissatisfactions with the administration of existing governmental programs. This is evident, for example, in the case of the refunding of internal revenue levies, and in the more recent controversy surrounding the withdrawal of public lands for the military services by the Department of the Interior. It is also reflected in the developments stemming from the dissatisfaction with the Interior Department's administration of the national wildlife refuges.

A second set of circumstances calling for committee clearance exists where the demands of certain programs have seemed to foreclose the possibilities of effective congressional control by any of the older and more traditional means. Into this category fell the naval construction programs during war time which called for fast and flexible decisions and actions. Such demands could not be met by the normal method of detailed and specific authorizations of funds for fairly long periods extending into the future. In order to meet the problems and at the same time provide an opportunity for congressional supervision of the use of general, lump-sum grants of funds, Congress established the device of prior committee approval. A similar situation underlay the more recent uses of this device in respect to construction of facilities and real estate acquisitions and disposals by the military services. In these cases committee clearance insured both flexibility in the conduct of these activities and effective means of congressional supervision.

The third set of circumstances in which recourse is had to this device involve congressional concern over new and untried governmental programs. Committee clearance has provided a means whereby Congress could establish such programs and maintain a close scrutiny over their initial execution. Examples are the new program of lease-purchase contracts for acquiring needed building space, and the program of government assistance in the construction of water retardation structures for irrigation and soil conservation.

The situations underlying the past establishment and use of committee clearance are bound to reappear in the future. They are not unique. The past uses of this device in such cases will undoubtedly not be lost to sight. It is reasonable to assume that such past experience and similar future circumstances will often lead to the reintroduction of committee clearance. To this extent, then, prior committee approval can be viewed as an addition to the instruments for congressional oversight of administrative discretion.

If this is true, it is necessary for students of the American governmental process to become thoroughly acquainted with the actual operation of this device. They must be able to evaluate dispassionately such a new governmental arrangement, and their judgment must be grounded upon a grasp of the administrative realities of any such arrangement. In order to establish this basis for evaluation, therefore, let us now turn to an analysis of the actual operation of committee clearance.

IV
COMMITTEE CLEARANCE OPERATION

The survey conducted in the last two chapters points out that the task of review and clearance of administrative decisions has been formally assigned to various organs of Congress. In one case a joint committee was charged with carrying out this function. In the larger number of instances a related committee in each chamber or a single committee of the lower house was given the responsibility of oversight. In one case, the review and clearance power was placed in the hands of a committee chairman. Given these statutory as well as informal arrangements, one might expect that the organs just referred to have actually been engaged in the study and approval or disapproval of administrative decisions.

This, however, has not been the case. These organs have normally played little or no part in the clearance process. There apparently are only three major exceptions to this generalization. One of these is the approval of the Bureau of the Budget bulletin by the House appropriation committee chairman. The chairman has been formally charged by statute with this responsibility, and he has continued to play the major role in review and clearance in this instance.[94] Clearance of particular Agriculture Department proposals by the Senate Committee on Agriculture and Forestry provides the second exception. This committee has been directed by statute to review and approve such department decisions, and it has retained this function in its own hands. The third exception involves the oversight by the House Committee on Interior and Insular Affairs of certain Interior Department decisions. This committee has continued to carry out the clearance function assigned to it by the 1957 statute. In every other case, however, the clearance of administrative decisions has not been carried out by the organ initially given this task by statute or agreement.

In all other cases, both those that are no longer operative and those that are still part of the national government scene, practice has led to de facto delegations of the clearance function to subordinate levels of the committee structure and even, in some cases, to individual members of the legislative body. There are three specific and distinguishable patterns of such delegation. In the first pattern the clearance of administrative decisions is left with a subcommittee and a member of the committee's professional staff. The second pattern is characterized by the delegation of the clearance function to the professional staff of the committee. In the third the scrutiny and approval of proposed decisions of executive agencies is actually delegated to individual members of Congress, who in most cases can not even claim membership on the reviewing committee.

---

94. The chairman often confers with other members of the committee before making a decision, but the final decision to approve or reject the proposed change always rests with the chairman. Interview with Mr. Sprankle, staff member, House Committee on Appropriations, January 7, 1957.

51

These are the realities of committee clearance. The remainder of this chapter is devoted to a detailed exposition of each of three patterns.

Patterns of Delegation

The first pattern of delegation is perhaps best represented by the reviewing practices followed by both armed services committees in the various instances of committee clearance, both formal and informal, in which they are presently involved. The decisions of the executive agencies--i.e., in most cases the military departments and the Department of Defense and, in a lesser number of instances, the Federal Civil Defense Administration--are submitted to both committees about once a week. The initial review of such decisions is performed by a regular member of the professional staff assigned to this duty. He prepares a short summary of the relevant data concerning each proposal. This summary is then submitted to a designated subcommittee along with the proposal. In the House of Representatives the proposals are submitted to a seven-member Subcommittee on Real Estate and Construction. In the case of the upper chamber they are submitted to a much smaller Subcommittee on Military Construction composed of three members. If the review by the staff member discloses no questions concerning the legality or reasonableness of the proposals they are generally approved by the subcommittees at periodic meetings with little detailed scrutiny. But if a question is raised by the staff member or a member of the subcommittee, a hearing is usually held by the subcommittee.[95]

---

95. Air Force Acquisition Project No. 99 of 1953, for instance, was the subject of a hearing by the predecessor of the present House subcommittee, the Subcommittee on Real Estate Acquisitions and Disposals. The Air Force previously had been authorized to purchase 760 acres of land at Carswell Air Force Base, Texas, for approximately 1.5 million

Representatives of the executive agency involved appear at such hearings to explain and justify the proposed action. Private parties that might be involved in the proposal--which is often the case in the acquisition or disposal of land or other real property--and interested members of Congress also usually present their views and urge the subcommittee to accept or reject the proposal or to modify it by inserting special requirements.[96] After accumulating the relevant facts and weighing the various issues that have been brought out by the hearing the subcommittee makes a decision concerning the disposition of the proposal.

The procedures of the two committees diverge after the subcommittee review is completed. In the case of the Senate, the Subcommittee on Military Construction has been authorized by the full Committee on Armed Services to make the final decision on each proposal that is submitted. The House armed services committee has not delegated this power to its subcommittee. The final disposition of each administrative decision is technically determined, therefore, by the full committee on the basis of subcommittee recommendations. This, however,

---

dollars. An earlier acquisition project to purchase 365 acres of this land, at a price of about 1.4 million dollars, had been approved by the House Committee on Armed Services in 1952. The Air Force proposed to obtain an additional 338 acres of the original authorization in Project No. 99 of 1953, but the price for this land had risen in the meantime to nearly 2.5 million dollars. This was an additional million dollars for a slightly lesser amount of land, and the subcommittee demanded an explanation. See U.S., Congress, House, Subcommittee on Real Estate Acquisitions and Disposals, 83d Cong., 1st Sess., 1953, A.S.P. No. 16.

96. See, for example, U.S., Congress, House, Subcommittee on Real Estate and Construction, 83d Cong., 1st Sess., 1953, A.S.P. No. 47 and A.S.P. No. 48.

is merely a matter of form; the subcommittee recommendations are almost invariably accepted. The full committee usually approves these proposals with little debate or consideration during meetings called to consider proposed bills or other legislative matters. The full House committee thus simply serves as the official organ for ratification of the decisions made at the subordinate levels of the committee structure.[97] In the clearance practice of the armed services committees, a subcommittee and a member of the professional staff, rather than the full committee, usually determine the dispositions of the proposals of the executive agencies.[98]

The same pattern of delegation was also employed in the clearance of lease-purchase contracts by the Senate Committee on Public Works during the time it was engaged in the oversight procedure.[99] The proposed lease-purchase contracts submitted to the Senate Committee on Public Works by the administrator of the General Services Administration and the Postmaster General were first reviewed by a member of the profes-

---

97. The information concerning the procedures of the armed services committees was obtained from personal interviews with Mr. Robert Smart, chief counsel, House Committee on Armed Services, January 2, 1957, and Mr. Harry L. Wingate, Jr., chief clerk, Senate Committee on Armed Services, January 7, 1957. See also Kofmehl, op. cit., supra, Chapter One, n. 2, pp. 209-211.

98. In the routine cases the actual decisions may be made by the staff member with the subcommittee serving merely to ratify such decisions without independent scrutiny. The point here is, however, that every case of committee clearance, whether routine or controversial, is actually carried out by the subcommittee and professional staff member rather than by the full committee.

99. The clearance practice of the House Committee on Public Works established a different pattern of delegation. It is discussed below. See infra, p.

sional staff. This staff member analyzed the proposals and prepared a memorandum on each one, summarizing the relevant data. These summaries were, in turn, submitted for review to a Subcommittee on Public Buildings and Grounds, composed of seven members. After such subcommittee review, which was based primarily upon the summary prepared by the staff member, the subcommittee arrived at recommendations of approval or disapproval of each project and submitted such recommended decisions to the full committee. The full committee almost invariably incorporated the subcommittee recommendations as its official decisions and, in this manner, served merely to ratify the choices arrived at by the staff member and the subcommittee.[100]

The same delegation pattern is evident in the clearance procedure established by the Senate Committee on Interior and Insular Affairs, which has been directed by a 1957 statute to review and approve proposed plans of financial assistance for the construction of small reclamation projects drawn up by the Department of the Interior. In this case the departmental proposals are submitted to the Subcommittee on Irrigation and Reclamation. The Committee Assistant for Reclamation, a member of the professional staff, is charged with assisting this subcommittee by performing the initial

---

100. Interview with Mr. T. W. Sneed, staff member, Senate Committee on Public Works, January 7, 1957. The procedure followed by the House Committee on Appropriations during the two brief periods in which it was charged with reviewing particular Defense Department decisions also produced an arrangement which falls into this first pattern. The full committee officially delegated the clearance power to its Subcommittee on Department of Defense Appropriations. This subcommittee, assisted by a staff member, made the final decisions concerning the department proposals. (The person who furnished this information in an interview at Washington, D.C., on January 7, 1957, requested that he remain anonymous.)

review of each proposal. His findings are then submitted to the subcommittee during its regular meetings. If the subcommittee has any questions or reservations about any proposed decision, the Bureau of Reclamation, as the agency in the Interior Department most directly concerned with such projects, is asked informally to clarify and justify the proposal, or a representative of the Bureau may be requested to appear at an open hearing held for such purpose. After scrutiny and possible hearing, the subcommittee arrives at a decision concerning the disposition of each department proposal. The decision is embodied in a resolution of approval or disapproval which is then submitted to the full committee. The full committee almost invariably adopts the subcommittee resolution as its own and forwards it to the Secretary of the Interior.[101]

The reviewing practices associated with the review of proposed tax refunds by the Joint Committee on Internal Revenue Taxation result in another pattern of delegation. The clearance of the refunds is performed almost exclusively by the professional staff of the joint committee. Neither the full committee nor a subcommittee is actively involved in the clearance practice.

The proposed refunds of the Internal Revenue Service are initially submitted to a staff office of the joint committee, which is located in the same building that houses the office of the Commissioner of Internal Revenue. The staff office is composed of a director and three attorneys whose sole duty it is to review refunds. A report of the initial review carried out by this office is

---

101. Letter from Mr. Goodrich W. Lineweaver, Committee Assistant for Reclamation, Senate Committee on Interior and Insular Affairs, dated January 21, 1959. The Senate subcommittee passed upon only six projects during the 85th Congress. The House interior committee follows a different procedure. See infra, p.

submitted to the chief of staff of the joint committee. If the initial reviewing staff and the chief of staff agree with the Internal Revenue Service concerning the proposals, final clearance for such refunds is given by the chief of staff. If they oppose the proposed refund, however, the chief of staff arranges a conference between representatives of the Internal Revenue Service and the staff of the joint committee. At this time the facts and the issues of the case are discussed in detail. Generally, agreement is reached at this level. Some refunds are, at this point, allowed to become effective while others are disallowed by the Internal Revenue Service in accordance with the wishes of the joint committee staff. Only the limited number of cases in which agreement cannot be reached are forwarded to the Joint Committee on Internal Revenue Taxation.

Such cases are submitted to an executive session of the joint committee. Representatives of the Internal Revenue Service appear at the meeting to present their views and justifications for the proposed refund. The arguments opposing such a refund are outlined by the joint committee staff. After weighing the various issues and arguments presented by both sides, the joint committee approves or disapproves each refund by a majority vote.

This formal committee vote, in the great majority of cases, upholds the position of the joint committee staff. Even in the small number of cases in which the joint committee takes an active role, therefore, the influence of the professional staff generally predominates in the committee disposition of the proposed refund. The joint Committee on Internal Revenue Taxation, sitting in an appellate capacity, almost always serves primarily to put the stamp of finality upon the initial decision of the professional staff.[102]

---

102. Interview with Mr. Colin Stam, chief of staff, Joint Committee on Internal Revenue Taxation, January 10, 1957.

The third pattern of delegation is followed by both committees on government operations in clearing the proposed negotiated disposals of surplus property by the General Services Administration or its designated agent. The reviewing practices, in the case of both of these committees, have led to the de facto delegation of the power of nullification of administrative decisions to individual members of Congress.

When the committees receive a proposed disposal from the executive branch, it is initially reviewed by a member of the professional staff of each committee to ascertain whether the disposal meets certain technical requirements. In the case of the House committee, the proposal is then referred, for consideration, to the congressman in whose district the surplus property is located. The Senate government operations committee similarly notifies the senators representing the state in which such property is located.[103] If the representative or senators have any objections to the disposal, they notify their respective committees within the established thirty-day laying period. Such objections almost invariably result in automatic disapproval of the proposal by the committee.[104] Both committees have thus established an inter-

---

See also Kofmehl, op. cit., supra, Chapter One, n. 2, pp. 206-208.

103. In some cases, of course, the property may be of such a nature as not to be located in a particular geographical area, as, for example, in the proposed disposal by the Air Force of sixty C-46F aircraft during the Eighty-third Congress. See "Activities of the Senate Committee on Government Operations" for the Eighty-third Congress, 84th Cong., 1st Sess., 1955, Senate Report No. 4, p. 28. In such a case the committees generally would make a decision based upon staff study and recommendation.

104. In the Eighty-fourth Congress, for example, the Interior Department proposed to exchange 3,861.01 acres of federal

esting system of "congressional courtesy" in which the actual power of nullification rests with individual members of the legislative body.[105]

The reviewing practices that were set up by the House Committee on Public Works for the clearance of proposed lease-purchase contracts resulted in similar delegation of the power of disapproval to individual members of the lower house. In this case, as in the case of both government operations committees, the clearance of administrative decisions rested primarily with individual members of Congress who generally could not even claim membership on the reviewing committee.

When proposed lease-purchase contracts were submitted to the House committee they were given an initial cursory review by a member of the professional staff. This was not a detailed review, however, for the committee was not equipped with a staff adequate to devote a great deal of time and attention to a thorough analysis and investigation of all the projects. After such staff review, the congressman from the area involved was notified about the proposed construction. The House public works committee relied primarily upon the recommendation of the congressman in arriving at its decision. If the House

---

property appraised at $272,000, and adjacent to Olympic National Park in Western Clallam and Jefferson Counties, Washington, for 400 acres of privately owned land, appraised at $269,350, in Lassen Volcanic National Park, Plumas County, California (plus $2,670 cash). "This proposal was objected to by the Senators from the state of Washington, and was not consummated by the Department of the Interior." "Activities of the Senate Committee on Government Operations" for the Eighty-fourth Congress, 85th Cong., 1st Sess., 1957, Senate Report No. 1, p. 46.

105. Interview with Mr. Walter L. Reynolds, chief clerk and staff director, Senate Committee on Government Operations, January 11, 1957.

member objected to the proposed building, the committee would disapprove the proposed contract. On the other hand, committee approval usually followed as a matter of course if the congressman in the area involved raised no objections to the proposed building.[106]

The House Committee on Agriculture has also followed this practice for the clearance of the Agriculture Department's proposals concerning plans of assistance to water and soil conservation districts constructing watershed projects. The reviewing practices that have been established by this committee, as in the case of the House public works committee and both Committees on Government Operations, have resulted in a de facto delegation of the clearance of administrative decisions to individual members of Congress. Whenever the committee receives a proposed plan of assistance, it is given a brief review by a member of the professional staff. The staff member then notifies the representative from the district in which the proposed project is to be built. The committee passes the necessary resolution of approval only if the proposed plan is acceptable to this member of the House.[107]

---

106. Interview with Mr. Robert F. McConnell, committee counsel, House Committee on Public Works, January 11, 1957. No detailed information was available concerning the procedure associated with the clearance of proposed decisions of the Interior Department relating to the national wildlife refuges. This has been carried out by the House Committee on Merchant Marine and Fisheries. It was discovered, however, that the House committee relies primarily upon the objections or approval of members of Congress. This is similar to the practice of the House public works committee. Interview with Mr. John M. Drewry, committee counsel, House Committee on Merchant Marine and Fisheries, January 5, 1957.

107. Interview with Mr. John Heimburger, committee counsel, House Committee on Agriculture, January 15, 1957.

The third pattern of delegation, then, puts the clearance function in the hands of people outside the committee structure itself. The actual power of nullification rests with individual members of Congress. The official decisions by the full committees to accept or reject an administrative decision, in any given case, represent little more than a ratification of the decisions made by the congressional members. As in the two patterns of delegation discussed previously, therefore, the full committees play only a minor role in the clearance process.[108]

The oversight arrangement with respect to the supervision of public land withdrawals by the House interior committee represented a rather special case. It cannot be completely fitted into any of the three delegation patterns discussed above. This becomes clear from a summary portrayal of the reviewing procedure. Whenever notice of a proposed withdrawal was received at the committee's office, a staff member would notify the governor of the state, as well as the House member or members from the area in which the public land was located, of the pending proposal. If none of these persons objected to the withdrawal, the committee simply issued an official committee approval. But if any of these individuals disagreed with the proposal, the House committee held a hearing. After such a hearing the commit-

---

108. The arrangement established by the Senate Committee on Appropriations for supervising Defense Department proposals also fits into this third pattern. In this instance, however, the clearance function was not entrusted to members of the chamber in general, but was rather limited to committee members. The necessary committee approval was granted unless a member objected to any proposal. In case of such objection a notification of committee disapproval was sent to the Defense Department. Interview with Mr. Cooper and Mr. Hewitt, staff members, Senate Committee on Appropriations, January 15, 1957.

tee arrived at an independent decision to validate or reject the particular withdrawal.

Thus, when the committee was faced with unanimous approval by the congressmen and governor, it simply became a pro forma ratifying body. But, whenever there was an objection by one of these governmental officials, the committee took an active part in the review of the proposals and made the final decisions itself. At times the procedure conformed to the third delegation pattern. At other times it proved an exception to all three categories discussed above.[109]

There apparently are only two cases in which a committee that has been originally charged with the oversight function has retained an active and independent role in the approval and disapproval of all submitted administrative decisions. The first involves the Senate Committee on Agriculture and Forestry, which has been engaged in the clearance process since 1954. This committee, along with its counterpart in the lower chamber, has been directed to review and approve proposed contracts, entered into by the Department of Agriculture, for federal aid to local watershed construction projects. Unlike the House committee, the Senate agriculture committee has continued to scrutinize and pass upon each of the proposals submitted by the Department of Agriculture.

The clearance procedure operates in the following manner. The proposed contracts submitted to the committee are given an initial review by the chief clerk of the committee. He prepares, for the benefit of the committee members, a short summary of the information relevant to each of the proposals. The committee then meets to

---

109. Interview with Mr. George Abbott, Committee counsel, House Committee on Interior and Insular Affairs, January 10, 1957.

consider the projects. If, after such committee consideration, none of the members have any serious question about a given Agriculture Department decision, the committee puts its stamp of approval upon the contracts. In case the committee feels it needs additional information in order to pass upon a project, or if reservations are raised, a hearing will be held before final decision. Representatives of the Agriculture Department appear at the hearing to explain and justify the projects. Officials of other executive agencies that administer programs closely related to the watershed construction program, such as the Bureau of Reclamation and the Army Corps of Engineers, also generally come before the committee to present their views and arguments.[110] The decisions to approve or reject the proposed projects are then made by the full committee on the basis of the information obtained at the hearing.[111]

The second case of an active committee grew out of the early 1957 statute requiring clearance of certain Interior Department decisions by the Committees on Interior and Insular Affairs. The House interior committee, in this instance, has so far reviewed the few proposals sent to it--totaling only six for the 85th Congress--and has reached its own independent decision concerning each one.

The Interior Department's decisions embodying proposed plans of financial assistance for small reclamation projects are submitted to the House committee, where they

110. See "Watershed Projects," Hearings before the Committee on Agriculture and Forestry, United States Senate, 84th Cong., 2d Sess., 1956.

111. Interview with Mr. Harker T. Stanton, committee counsel, Senate Committee on Agriculture and Forestry, January 7, 1957, and letter dated January 6, 1959, from Mr. Cotys M. Mouser, Chief Clerk, Senate Committee on Agriculture and Forestry.

are initially reviewed by the Consultant on Irrigation
and Reclamation Matters, a member of the professional
staff. The committee takes up the consideration of these
proposals at a regular committee meeting. At such
a meeting the committee consultant or a representative
of the Department of Interior testifies briefly on each
project in regard to technical matters, such as cost,
feasibility, and repayment. Committee members then
are given the opportunity to ask questions about the proposals. After the members feel sufficiently briefed on
each contemplated contract, a committee decision is
made on each Interior Department proposal.[112]

The reviewing practices of the Senate agriculture committee and the House interior committee have not de-
generated into pro forma ratification. Both stand out as
major exceptions to the general trend toward delegation
of the review power.

---

112. Letter from Mr. Sidney L. McFarland, Engineering Con-
     sultant, House Committee on Interior and Insular Affairs,
     dated January 17, 1959.

V
COMMITTEE CLEARANCE: AN EVALUATION

A brief appraisal of committee clearance will have to begin with a delineation of the major advantages and defects of prior committee approval. It will then be possible to weigh the favorable aspects against the shortcomings in order to render a final judgment.

In several respects, this device can be applauded. In the first place, it subjects administrative decisions to a final review and scrutiny by sources unconnected with the execution of a given governmental program. Irrespective of the persons or agencies actually carrying out the review function, there is an inherent virtue in such a procedure. It requires proposed decisions to pass the scrutiny of complex values, orientations, and perspectives, which generally will be different from that serving as the decisional premise of the executive agency.

The agency is necessarily identified with the administration of a governmental program and concerned about

the successful accomplishment of the statutory mandate.
This, of course, is its raison d'etre. The organizational
context is liable to induce selectivity in decision-making;
particularistic perspectives and values are magnified
while more general problems and probable consequences
are neglected or overlooked. Scrutiny and review by
individuals less closely connected with the agency, and
who hold what is essentially a "lay" point of view, will
more than likely point out and emphasize such problems
and consequences of administrative proposals.

A second major advantage of prior committee approval
is that it furnishes a possible supplemental means of
legislative control of administrative discretion that can
be used in those instances in which the normal methods
are generally impotent and ineffective. These particular instances are increasing day by day in the contem-
porary administrative process and are rapidly becoming
commonplace. More and more often, Congress finds it
necessary to vest broad and loosely circumscribed discretionary authority in executive agencies; the demands
for government programs and action in modern day
America make this mandatory. It is virtually impossible
for the legislature, in such instances, to draw up a
framework of detailed and precise standards which can
serve to channel and circumscribe the uses of such
powers. Correspondingly, the specific exercises of
such broad authority tend to become a matter of the
highest concern to the legislature, and it is recognized
that any real degree of congressional control must come
through control of these specific uses.

This, however, is precisely where problems arise.
Congressional control has generally taken the form of
traditional and well-known techniques of periodic investigations, review and censure, and annual budgetary
scrutiny. These are not effective methods of day-to-day
control. They are postnatal and ex post facto in nature
and thus have only limited usefulness. Such techniques

can simply provide a means of challenging past exercises of delegated powers, which are faits accomplis, and of reorienting future uses by general instructions and threats. The one thing they cannot accomplish is current supervision and control of the uses of delegated authority.

The very failure of the normal surveillance techniques to provide the necessary degree of control when it is actually most needed points up the usefulness of committee clearance for Congress. The device provides for just such occasions a way whereby Congressional committees, acting as agents of the legislative body, can scrutinize each and every proposed use of the authority entrusted to executive agencies and can determine whether it should become effective. It thus furnishes Congress with a stand-by device which can be put into operation in instances where a close control over specific administrative decisions is desired but unobtainable through the traditional methods of legislative supervision.

A third advantage of committee clearance is one which accrues to the executive agencies charged with the exercise of delegated powers in the administration of government programs. Such powers are granted and the programs sanctioned by Congress, either with the approval of the President or over his objections. The favorable reaction of the legislature to the uses of the delegated authority and the administration of the programs is thus necessarily of major concern to the agencies. Unfavorable reaction can very easily lead to recrimination through the budget process, embarrassing and trying legislative investigations, statutory revision-- perhaps even elimination of the program. The security and stability of the agencies and their programs, then, depend to a great extent on the calculation and prediction of congressional reaction.

Committee clearance helps to decrease the guesswork in such calculations and predictions and, in this manner, promotes security and stability. By requiring that each use of delegated powers must be accompanied by congressional committee acceptance, it assures the agencies of approval and support by the most influential units of the legislative branch. This will in almost all cases reduce the possibility of later legislative recrimination. In view of the gain in the security and stability of executive agencies and administrative programs, it is possible that this device is not entirely unwelcome to the agencies of the executive branch.

These are important advantages. They should not be dismissed lightly. Before they can be properly assessed, however, they must be weighed against a single basic defect of the committee oversight scheme.

Committee clearance strips both the chief executive and the legislative body of any official role in the final supervision of the uses of discretionary powers of the regular executive agencies. Neither of these major organs is actively engaged in the review and clearance function. The actual operation of this device, as we have seen, places this function at several other points in the governmental structure. In three instances, it has been carried out by congressional committees. In the larger number of cases, it has been placed in the hands of subcommittees and the professional staff of committees, and sometimes even in the hands of individual congressmen. The committees, in such cases, have generally served simply as pro forma ratifying organs.

This circumvention of both the President and Congress represents a departure from the normal rule underlying arrangements for the control of administrative discretion. This rule is generally unverbalized. When put into words, however, it reads something like this: The uses of the discretionary authority entrusted to the major executive agencies must be subject in some fashion or other to the ultimate supervision of either the presidency or the legislature. This particular directive is manifest, for example, in the principle of presidential power to remove the heads of the executive departments; it is through such a sanction that the discretionary powers found within these departments are brought under the ultimate direction and control of the chief executive. The rule is also reflected in the many cases in which the President is by statute formally assigned the final review and approval of particular decisions of subordinate executive agencies. This same rule also underlies the more recent practice of placing final clearance of administrative decisions in the hands of Congress through the use of the resolution procedure, a practice which focuses on the legislature rather than the presidency as the proper organ of review and control.

The reason behind this standard is not difficult to uncover. It has its basis in the recognition that the exercise of delegated discretionary authority by the executive agencies generally does not involve simply the technical and noncontroversial implementation of government policies worked out by the President and Congress and put into statute form. The administrative decisions go far beyond this. They are actually the instruments for building direction and specific meaning into the general, and normally rather vague and ambiguous, policy pronouncements and declarations contained in the statutory mandates. They are, in short, like the statutes themselves, policy decisions and are thus an integral part of the government policy-making process.

One of the basic and most revered ideals of our political ideology is that the will of the people must guide and circumscribe the formulation of public policy. If, then, this rule is going to continue to operate in regard to the more specific aspects of government policy-making as well as its general outlines, it is necessary that the final control of the exercise of administrative discretion shall rest with the governmental organ that best reflects and represents this popular will. The legacy of American thought about government administration has bestowed the honor of being the most appropriate organ for such purpose upon both the President and Congress.

There is good reason, therefore, for allowing some form of ultimate supervision by either the chief executive or the legislature. Such an arrangement, according to American administrative theory, permits the implementation of a basic principle underlying our governmental system. This principle is expressed in brief terms as the demand that the making of public policy must rest upon the consent of the governed. [113]

This pattern of thought, once spelled out clearly, points up the basic failure of committee clearance. This device replaces the President and Congress with other points of supervision and control of administrative discretion-- committees, subcommittees, professional staff, and congressmen--which are almost unanimously recognized as inadequate and unacceptable sources for the determination and translation of the popular will. The final clearance decisions--i.e., the approval and nullification of administrative decisions--stemming from these points in the governmental structure cannot be upheld as valid

---

113. It should be mentioned at this point that there is a question as to whether committee clearance is constitutional. There have been no court cases specifically concerning this device, however, and the arguments that have been offered to uphold its constitutionality or to deny its validity are inconclusive. Moreover, a close study of past judicial decisions relating to the pertinent constitutional language shows that a strong case can be made to support either side of this issue. For a detailed analysis of this problem see William E. Rhode, "Congressional Review of Administrative Decision-Making by Committee Clearance and Resolutions," Chapter IX, (Michigan State University Library, 1958).

and satisfactory approximations of the consent of the governed. In the final analysis, therefore, committee clearance establishes an arrangement which has built into it a violation of the fundamental principle that governmental policy-making must reflect and represent the total community consensus.

The belief that policy decisions of our government should rest upon and reflect the consent of the governed is a basic principle in the complex of American political ideals. Its attainment in our governmental structure and process is considered of paramount importance, and, by the same token, the failure to meet this standard is looked upon as a grave indictment of any governmental arrangement. The fact that committee clearance does not live up to this principle therefore stands as a serious argument against it. It takes on far more importance than the several advantages listed and discussed previously, which become rather superficial and insignificant in comparison.

The choice is thus clearly drawn. We can accept committee clearance only if we are willing to barter away one of our most cherished ideals for what become, by comparison, surface advantages. Few would agree to such an exchange. The final conclusion, therefore, must be that committee clearance is an improper and invalid addition to the repertory of instruments for the control of administrative discretion in the American national government system.

Politics in the Press: An Analysis of Press Content in 1952 Senatori
Campaigns. 1954. LeRoy C. Ferguson and Ralph H. Smuckler.
 An analysis of press content in the 1952 senatorial campaig
 in Connecticult and Wisconsin.   Cloth $2.
               Paper $1.

Leadership and Participation in Urban Political Affairs.   195
Ralph H. Smuckler and George M. Belknap.
 An investigation of the relationship between types of issues a
 the involvement of various leadership groups in the local con
 community.   Paper $.

How They Became Governor. 1957. Joseph A. Schlesinger.
 The political careers of all Governors elected in the U.S. betwe
 1870 and 1950.   Paper $1.

The Michigan One-Man Grand Jury. 1957. Robert G. Scigliani
 Michigan's unique experiment in the administration of justi
 described as part of the political process.   Paper $1.

Policy Change in Prison Management. 1957. Richard H. McCleer
 A study of communication processes and regimes in two penite
 tiaries considered as small scale political communities.
               Paper $.

Quantitative Analysis of Judicial Behavior. In press, Spring 195
Glendon A. Schubert.
 The first extensive exploration of the voting of Supreme Cou
 Justices and other judges by means of statistical observatio
 scaling and other techniques. (Order from The Free Pres
 Glencoe, Ill.)   Cloth $7.

Civic Education in the United States: A Directory. 1954. Robe
Horwitz and Carl Tjerandsen.
 A directory of organizations active in this field.
               Cloth $3.

1958-59 Supplement to Civic Education in the United States:
Directory. 1959. Robert Horwitz and Carl Tjerandsen.
               Cloth $2.